From the Editors and Contributors of *Threads*
A *SewStylish* publication

This material was previously published by *Threads*.
See page 32 for Credits. All rights reserved.
First published in this format 2012

Cover Photographer: Scott Phillips

Editor: Deana Tierney May
Art Director: Rosann Berry
Senior Technical Editor: Judith Neukam
Special Issue Technical Editor: Carol Fresia
Associate Editors: Sarah McFarland, Stephani L. Miller
Central Staff Editor: Sarah Opdahl
Senior Copy/Production Editor: Jeanine Clegg
Assistant Art Director: Gloria Melfi
Administrative Assistant: April Mohr
Seamstress: Norma Bucko
Executive Editor, Series: Shawna Mullen

threadsmagazine.com
Executive Web Producer: Victoria North
Web Producer: Evamarie Gomez

Taunton's SewStylish (ISSN: 1935-8482) is published by
The Taunton Press Inc., Newtown, CT 06470-5506.
Telephone 203-426-8171

The Taunton Press
Inspiration for hands-on living®

The Taunton Press, Inc., 63 South Main Street, PO Box 5506,
Newtown, CT 06470-5506
e-mail: tp@taunton.com

Library of Congress Cataloging-in-Publication Data in progress

ISBN: 978-1-62113-831-0

Printed in the United States of America
10 9 8 7 6 5 4 3 2 1

Contents

Easy Beaded Bags

Here's the perfect project for your favorite bold, patterned fabrics. Choose two fat quarters (18-inch by 22-inch rectangles of fabric), and you'll have the perfect amount to make one dimensional and one flat bag. Find a great print, preferably in a large scale to make a more dramatic statement, and then use quilting and beading techniques to play off the patterns in a creative way. Batik prints' beautiful designs can lay the groundwork for the quilting and beading steps. Once you've chosen fabrics and carefully planned out the placement of the print, you can make a bag in just a couple of hours.

These bags are a super way to squeeze in some quilting when you don't have the time to commit to making a full-scale quilt. These bags also offer a great opportunity to practice zipper installation without too much investment. Plus, you can make the bags as simple or as elaborate as you like.

DEBBIE CORSON *is a contributor to* SewStylish.

Supplies

- Batting, thin and lightweight, ½ yard
- Clear plastic ruler
- Beading needle (I prefer size 13)
- Iron
- Marking pen
- Point turner
- Quilting fabric, batik or other large-scale print, two fat quarters (18-by-22-inch rectangles)
- Seed beads (in 7 to 10 colors)
- Sewing machine
- Scissors or rotary cutter
- Thread, for sewing and beading
- Zipper, 7 inches long
- Zipper foot

tip **BEAUTY INSIDE AND OUT**

Solid color fabric may be less expensive, but printed fabric linings can lend a fun, surprising quality to a bag.

Quilt, bead, and sew

To make a medium-size bag (5½ inches by 7½ inches), first cut and layer the fabric, and then machine-quilt. Next, add a zipper and follow by sewing around the edges of the bag. Finally, make the bag dimensional, and then bead it. Try adding a bead at every other machine stitch.

1 LAYER, PIN, AND CUT YOUR FABRIC. On a flat surface, lay the lining fabric wrong-side up. Lay the batting over it, and then lay the outer fabric on top, right-side up. Copy the pattern on page 4, place it on top of the fabric, and use a rotary cutter or scissors to cut out the layered pieces. Repeat for the second side of the bag.

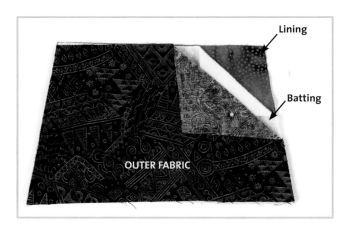

Lining

Batting

OUTER FABRIC

Patterns & Templates

Here are the templates and patterns you'll need to create some these bags. Before making copies of any patterns or templates, check the accuracy of your photocopier by making one copy and comparing it to the original. Permission granted to copy patterns and templates for personal use.

Copy these templates to create the beaded bags. We copied ours at 400 percent.

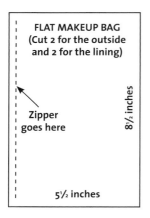

FLAT MAKEUP BAG
(Cut 2 for the outside and 2 for the lining)

Zipper goes here

8½ inches

5½ inches

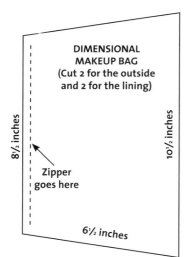

DIMENSIONAL MAKEUP BAG
(Cut 2 for the outside and 2 for the lining)

8½ inches

10½ inches

Zipper goes here

6½ inches

2 MACHINE-QUILT THE LAYERS. Pin through the layers at the corners. Free-motion-quilt each piece in a design that complements the outer fabric's print. Backstitch at the beginning and end of each line or shape. For patterns with tight turns, you may want to use a zipper foot.

Quilt line

3 PREP FOR THE ZIPPER. With right sides together, pin the quilted bag-front and bag-back pieces along the top edge, and machine-baste them together with ⅝-inch seam allowances. Next, press both layered pieces while they're still flat. Then, open the two layered pieces, fold open the seam allowance, and press. Finally, press the seam again from the right side

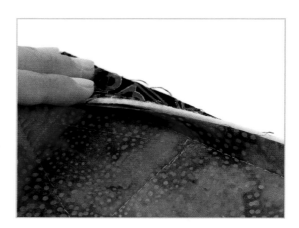

4 ADD THE ZIPPER. Pin the zipper over the seam allowance on the wrong side. Make sure it is centered over the basting stitches. Hand-baste the zipper, and remove the pins. Install a zipper foot on your machine, and align it with the outer edge of the zipper tape. Then stitch evenly along each side.

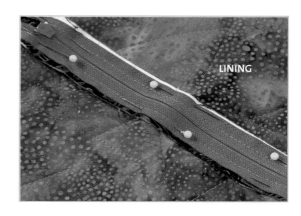

LINING

5 **PRESS, AND THEN REMOVE THE MACHINE BASTING.** Press near the zipper on the right side. Use a seam ripper to remove the basting threads over the zipper.

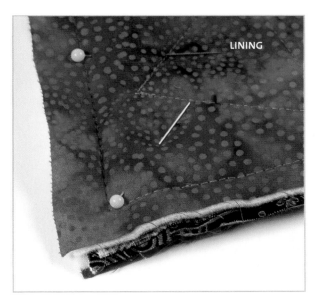

6 **SEW THE BAG.** First, unzip the zipper. Then, pin the sides, and bag the bottom edges right sides together. Stitch around the edge of the bag with a $5/8$-inch seam allowance, starting on one end of the zipper and finishing on the other. Trim seam allowances to $1/4$ inch, and zigzag the edges together.

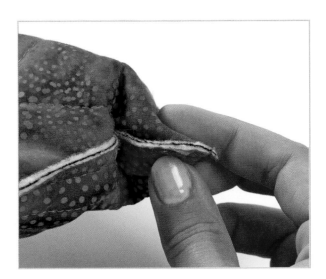

7 **SHAPE THE BOTTOM.** To add dimension to the bag, bend the tip of each bottom corner toward the bottom seam, draw a line across the exposed side of the bend $1/4$ inch below the very tip, and pin it in place. Hand-stitch along the line, trim off the excess corner fabric, and zigzag. Turn the bag right-side out, and use a point turner to make the corners neat.

8 **BEAD THE BAG.** Thread a beading needle, and knot the thread end. Pull the thread through from the inside of the bag. Stitch beads onto the outside, following the path of the quilting stitches. You don't need to stitch through the bag after the first stitch; just catch the quilting stitches, and add one bead at a time.

Pretty Pincushions

Are you ready for "oohs" and "ahs" all around? At just 1½ inches tall, these minute pincushions will be the darlings of any party and the apple of any craftster's eye. They fit neatly into a sewing box and are extremely handy perched on a sewing machine (just add a Velcro dot). And for friends who haven't yet caught the sewing bug, these itty bitty cushions are the perfect addition to a jewelry box: they corral earrings and pins in high style.

These cushions are a blast to make and use recycled material: The base is a soda-bottle cap wrapped with craft felt. As you can see at left, from there, the sky's the limit in terms of design. Besides simple shapes reminiscent of cupcakes or candy, you can fashion a mini poinsettia, a crown, or even a beehive or cactus—cute, cuter, cutest!

JEN SEGREST *is a web designer who lives in southwestern Ohio.*

Supplies

- Plastic cap from a liter-size soda bottle
- Chalk
- Sharp scissors
- Craft felt
- Large-eye embroidery needle
- Multicolored skeins of embroidery floss
- Poly fiberfill

Build it from the base up

The final pincushion size will be 1½ by 1¼ inches. In the steps below, use a single knotted piece of embroidery floss. To ensure quick, knotless sewing, don't trim the floss after each step.

1 CUT THE BASE. Lay the bottle cap on a small square of felt. Trace the shape with chalk. Then cut along the chalk line with sharp scissors.

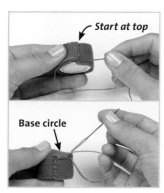

Start at top

Base circle

2 CUT THE OUTER SLEEVE, AND SEW IT TO THE BASE. Cut a felt strip a bit wider than your cap's height and long enough to wrap around the cap with some overlap. Wrap it around the cap. Then slipstitch along the overlap. Pop in the base circle, and slipstitch around it as shown. Don't cut the floss!

Gather

3 MAKE THE BALL TOP. Cut a 3-inch square, and then round the corners. Baste around the circle's outer edge. Pull the floss ends to gather. Stuff the pouch with poly fiberfill (until the ball is hard), and knot the floss ends. Press the ball into the base.

Embroider just for fun

Pincushions are the perfect canvas for hand embroidery. Combine these stitches to make flowers, vines, or geometric designs. If at first you don't succeed, try again. Felt is very forgiving.

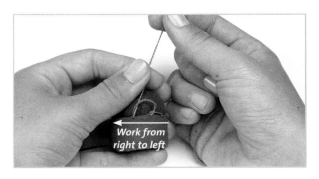

BLANKET STITCH

Use this stitch to secure the base and the top. Working from right to left, bring the needle from back to front ⅛ inch from the edge. Keep the thread from the previous stitch under the needle point.

FEATHER STITCH

Working from right to left, bring the needle out at point A. Insert it at point B, holding the thread to the left. Bring the needle up at point C over the thread. Point C then becomes point A. Repeat.

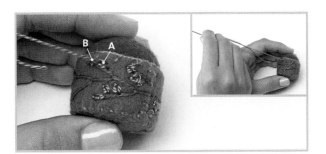

LAZY DAISY

Bring the needle out at point A. Reinsert it into the same hole or close to it, leaving a loop. Exit at point B, holding the loop under the needle. Pull the needle through. Insert the needle on other side of the thread loop.

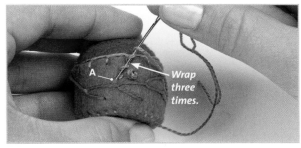

FRENCH KNOT

Bring the needle and thread out at point A. Hold the thread taut with your left hand, and wrap it around the needle two or three times. Insert the wrapped needle close to point A.

Tips for mass production

CUTTING AHEAD

Cut 3-inch squares from 9x12-inch sheets of craft felt. Then store the ready-to-use stack in your work area. The squares are the perfect size for pincushion bases, ball tops, and leaf or flower accents.

ASSEMBLY-LINE CONSTRUCTION

To make many pincushions, cut out the shapes first. Sew one step at a time on every cushion, and then move on to the next step. Use a long thread so that you can just cut it, and move on to the next cushion without rethreading.

Pillow Pom-Poms

Whether you're embellishing pillows, lamp shades or even making a brooch, pompoms add a fun and quirky touch to just about any project. You can completely transform a boring pillow with a fun, frothy fabric pompom.

With all the new tools available, making pompoms is surprisingly easy. But did you know that you can make them with materials other than yarn? Scrap fabrics are perfect for creating a raw but sophisticated look. We combined coordinating fabrics, but you can also use anything that you can wrap around the tool—try bits of roving, ribbon, trim, or raffia. You can even customize the pom-pom to any size or shape your crafty heart desires.

NICOLE SMITH *is a former associate editor at* Threads *magazine.*

Supplies

- Fabric, 1/8 yard
- Hand needle
- Pillow, 18-inch square
- Pompom maker (We used a large Clover Pom-Pom Maker)
- Scissors
- Thread

Make pom-poms from scraps

Fabric pompoms offer a sophisticated way to use up scraps and add a simple flourish anywhere you wish.

1 CUT FABRIC STRIPS. Cut fabric strips across the width of the fabric from selvage to selvage. You'll want two strips for each side of the pompom. At left, one strip is approximately ¾ inch wide and the second strip is approximately ½ inch wide.

2 WRAP THE STRIPS AROUND THE POMPOM MAKER. Following the tool's instructions, wrap two layered fabric strips around one side of the tool, as shown above. Wrap the two remaining fabric strips around the opposite side of the tool.

3 CUT AND FINISH THE POMPOM. Follow the tool's instructions to cut and finish the pompom. Hand-sew several stitches to secure the pompom to the pillow. Or, to make the pompom removable, sew on a pin backing to it.

Origami Pouches

Make the most of luscious fabrics. Even small remnants have the potential to become lovely little purses with this project. Folded from fabric squares, these adorable—and reversible—pouches can be cut and sewn in less than an hour. Not only will this project transform a fabric stash into gifts and accessories, it's a fantastic outlet for creative sewing. For a dressy event, make an evening bag. For day, use one as a wallet, and slip it into a larger carryall or briefcase.

Virtually any fabric will do. The pouches are gorgeous in velvet, satin, and silk dupioni. For a more casual look, try linen, cotton batiks, denim, or wool suitings. The only fabrics to avoid are very lightweight fabrics, sheers, and knits.

Adapted from "Mini Purses" by **PADDYE MANN** *in Threads issue 134.*

Supplies

- Fabric remnants for lining and pouch (sheers or knits are not recommended)
- 20 inches, or more, decorative cording to complement fabric
- Fabric marker
- Hand-sewing needle
- Iron and ironing board
- Paper for pattern
- Pen or pencil
- Scissors
- Sewing machine
- Thread

Optional:
- Decorative notions: embroidery thread, buttons
- Fusible interfacing (weight to go with fabric)

For Larger Bags
- Chipboard or cardboard
- Heavyweight interfacing

Make a square pattern

As with origami, you'll start off with a paper square. The pattern can be as large or as small as you desire. The patterns for the bags shown were based on office stationery and are 8½ inches, 11 inches, and 14 inches square (including ⅜-inch seam allowances) and yield bags from about 5 inches to just under 10 inches per side.

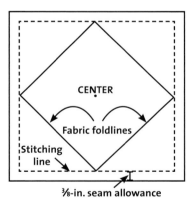

CENTER

Fabric foldlines

Stitching line

⅜-in. seam allowance

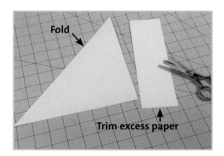

Fold

Trim excess paper

1 FOLD AND CUT THE PAPER.
Fold it diagonally to align a vertical and a horizontal edge (the fold bisects two opposite corners). Crease the fold. Trim any excess (single-layer) paper.

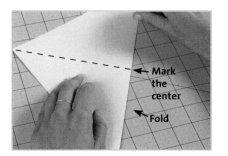

Mark the center

Fold

2 FOLD THE PAPER AGAIN.
Open the square. Fold and crease it diagonally between the uncreased corners. Mark the folds' intersection at the square's center.

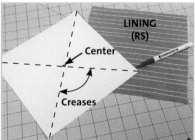

LINING (RS)

Center

Creases

3 CUT FABRIC AND LINING.
Use the pattern to cut a fashion fabric square and a lining square. Mark the pattern's center on the lining's right side with a fabric marker.

Sew it together

If necessary, reinforce the fabric and lining with fusible interfacing in a weight that's appropriate for the fabric. Cut and fuse the interfacing to each square's wrong side before you proceed to the following steps.

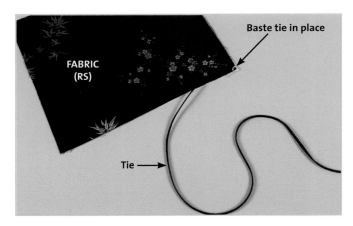

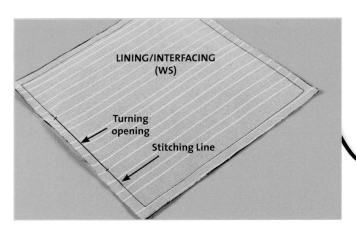

1 ADD A TIE TO ONE CORNER. Cut a 20-inch cord length. Place it on the fabric piece's right side, a cut end aligned with a raw-edged corner. Baste the tie in place.

2 JOIN THE FABRIC AND LINING. Layer the squares, right sides together, with the tie's length in the square's center. Stitch all around, catching the cord end in the corner and leaving a 2-inch opening on one side.

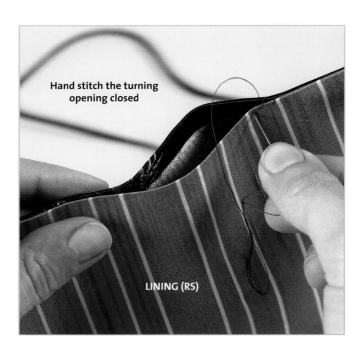

3 TURN AND PRESS THE PURSE. Clip the corners, then turn the work right side out through the opening, and press flat. Slipstitch the opening closed.

4 FORM THE BAG. Machine-edgestitch the square if desired. Fold the corners to the center marked on the lining. Hand-whipstitch two pairs of edges together.

Customize the pouch

The origami pouch can be constructed from all sorts of beautiful fabrics. It also offers many embellishment and finishing options. Try these details:

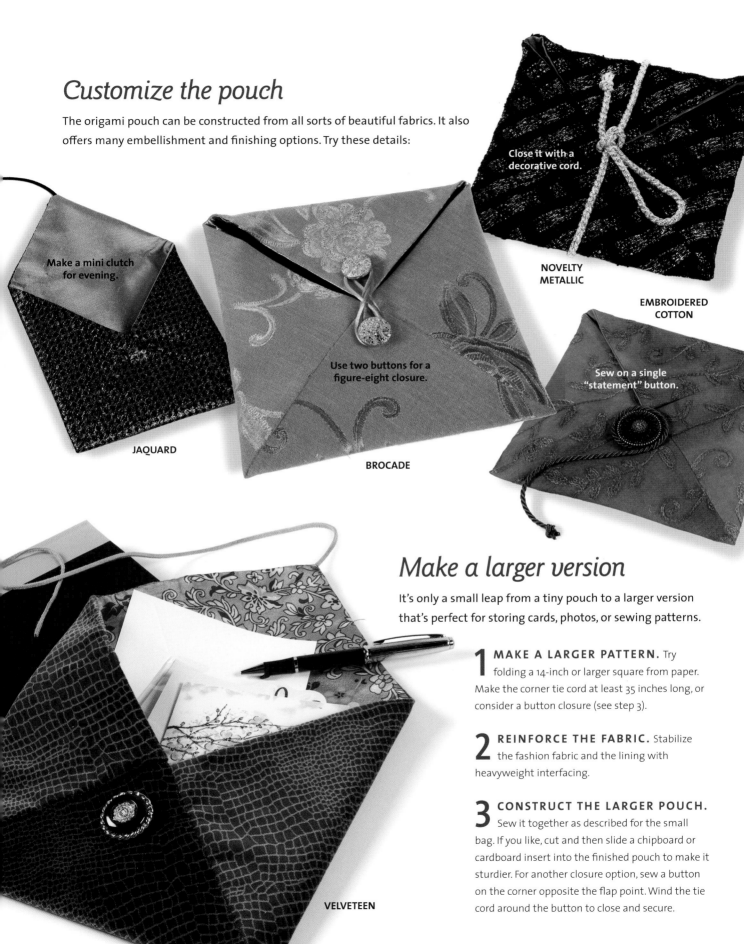

Make a mini clutch for evening.

Close it with a decorative cord.

Use two buttons for a figure-eight closure.

Sew on a single "statement" button.

JAQUARD

BROCADE

NOVELTY METALLIC

EMBROIDERED COTTON

VELVETEEN

Make a larger version

It's only a small leap from a tiny pouch to a larger version that's perfect for storing cards, photos, or sewing patterns.

1 MAKE A LARGER PATTERN. Try folding a 14-inch or larger square from paper. Make the corner tie cord at least 35 inches long, or consider a button closure (see step 3).

2 REINFORCE THE FABRIC. Stabilize the fashion fabric and the lining with heavyweight interfacing.

3 CONSTRUCT THE LARGER POUCH. Sew it together as described for the small bag. If you like, cut and then slide a chipboard or cardboard insert into the finished pouch to make it sturdier. For another closure option, sew a button on the corner opposite the flap point. Wind the tie cord around the button to close and secure.

Crescent Clutch

Felt goes glamorous with this simple-to-sew clutch. Wool felt has long been considered a fabric for kids because its resistance to fraying makes it one of the easiest materials to use. But it can also elevate a project beyond the everyday. Made from richly toned wool felt, this clutch feels lush, high-end, and completely grown-up. If felt doesn't suit you, this pattern can work with any sturdy fabric.

A fan-folded flap detail lends a modern touch to this clutch's simple half-moon shape. Sew on gems, fancy buttons, or vintage jewels—or pin on a few stunning brooches—to make a bag that's uniquely you!

ERIKA KERN is a crafter and sewer and runs Etsy.com/Shop/ MyImaginaryBoyfriend.

Supplies

- Fabric
  > 1 yard wool-blend felt
  > $\frac{1}{2}$ yard lining
- 1 package extra-wide ($\frac{1}{2}$-inch), double-fold bias tape
- Stabilizers
  > 1 yard fusible interfacing
  > 1 yard sew-in ultrafirm stabilizer
- Craft knife
- Iron
- Magnetic snap closure
- Pins
- Pliers
- Rotary cutter, grid, and mat
- Scissors (for paper and fabric)
- Sewing machine
- Sew-on gems, buttons, brooches
- Thread

Make the purse body

This clutch has a simple shape and uses just three pattern pieces: one for the body, one for the flap, and one for the flap stabilizer. All seam allowances are $\frac{3}{8}$ inch unless otherwise noted. (Find the pattern on page 30.)

CLUTCH BODY
Cut:
2 pieces felt and lining
2 pieces interfacing
2 pieces stabilizer

CLUTCH FLAP
Cut:
2 pieces felt
1 piece interfacing

CLUTCH FLAP STABILIZER
Cut 1

1 CUT THE CLUTCH PIECES FROM FELT, LINING, INTERFACING, AND STABILIZER. Choose a flap piece for the flap underside and a body piece for the clutch front. Mark the snap placement on the flap underside piece and on the front body piece.

3 ATTACH ONE HALF OF THE MAGNETIC CLOSURE TO THE FLAP UNDERSIDE. Center it about 1½ inches above the finished curved edge. Follow the snap manufacturer's instructions.

2 SEW THE FRONT FLAP. Trim fusible interfacing seam allowances, then fuse interfacing to the flap underside's wrong side. Pin both flap pieces, right sides together, and sew through the felt layers along the curved edge. Turn the flap right side out and press. Insert the ultrafirm stabilizer piece between the two flap layers; smooth the edges so they lie flat. Press.

Stitch along the flap's curved edge, catching all felt and fusible interfacing layers

4 PREPARE THE CLUTCH BODY. Iron each of the fusible interfacing body pieces to the wrong sides of both felt body pieces. On the front piece's right side, attach the magnetic closure's second half (centered about 1½ inches from the curved edge's seam allowance).

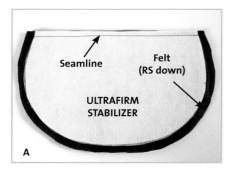

Seamline

Felt
(RS down)

ULTRAFIRM
STABILIZER

A

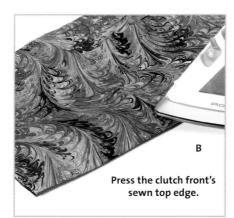

B

Press the clutch front's
sewn top edge.

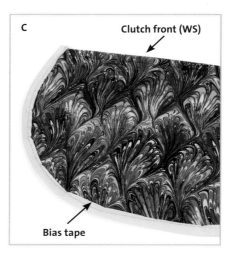

C

Clutch front (WS)

Bias tape

5 ASSEMBLE THE CLUTCH FRONT.

Layer the front body pieces together in the following order: lining (RS up), felt (RS down), and ultrafirm stabilizer. Sew together along the top edge (A). Trim the excess stabilizer along the seam allowance, turn right side out, and press (B). To finish the bottom raw edge, pin the edges together and sew through all layers within the seam allowance. Wrap bias tape over the curved edge to enclose all layers, pin, and edgestitch in place (C).

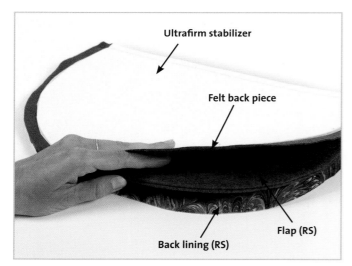

Ultrafirm stabilizer

Felt back piece

Back lining (RS)

Flap (RS)

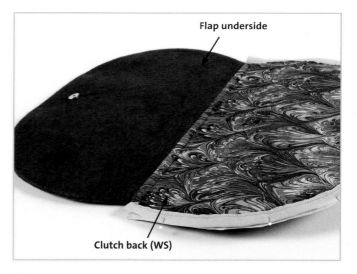

Flap underside

Clutch back (WS)

6 ATTACH THE FLAP TO THE CLUTCH BACK.

Layer the back body pieces and clutch flap in this order: back lining (RS up), clutch flap (RS up), back felt body piece (RS down), and ultrafirm stabilizer. Sew along the straight edge. Trim the excess stabilizer close to the seam allowance, turn right side out so the lining covers the stabilizer, and press the seam. Follow the directions for finishing the bottom edge in step 5.

7 ASSEMBLE THE CLUTCH.

Pin the clutch front to the clutch back, felt sides (RS) together, and sew them together along their curved edges. Turn the clutch right side out and press.

Add a folded flourish

A fan-fold detail dresses up the flap of this basic clutch.

1 CREATE THE FAN. Cut a felt rectangle 12 inches wide by 24 inches long. Fold the rectangle perpendicular to its length into a fan shape: overlapped at one end and spread out at the other.

2 EXPERIMENT WITH THE SHAPE. Making the folds wider or narrower changes the number of folds in the fan. Folding the felt repeatedly won't damage it.

3 ONCE YOU ACHIEVE THE DESIRED EFFECT, PRESS THE FELT TO SECURE THE FAN SHAPE. Hand-sew tacks under the folded edges to hold them in place.

4 ATTACH THE FAN TO THE CLUTCH FLAP. Pin, then hand-stitch the fan to the flap along the fan's top, bottom, and sides, hiding the stitches under the fan's edges.

Decorate the fan front

There are many options for decorating the fan treatment on your new clutch. To mix it up and match your outfits, apply sew-on gems, novelty beads or buttons, iron-on appliqués, silk or ribbon blossoms, or pin a beautiful brooch at either end of the fan. Use lighter-weight embellishments if you make the clutch smaller or in a lighter material.

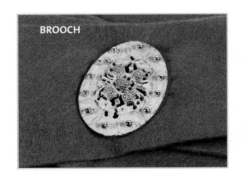

BROOCH

SEW-ON GEMS

NOVELTY BEADS

Collage Cards Galore

You can really never have too much fabric or too many note cards. If you have always loved having a stash of unusual cards for various occasions, here's your chance to start designing and creating your own. Collage is fun and a perfect technique for making note cards. They're a natural canvas for scraps of fabric and trim that are too beautiful to throw away. The process is really simple and doesn't have any rules. Just start snipping, gluing, and stitching, and let your creative juices flow!

Former Threads *editor* **CHRIS TIMMONS** *sews and teaches in Norwalk, Connecticut.*

Supplies

- Card stock
- Scissors and ruler
- Rotary cutter
- Bone folder
- Thread
- Fabric scraps
- 505 spray or glue stick

Make a blank card

Begin by cutting and folding a few blank cards out of heavy paper. Available at art-supply stores in various weights and in a range of neutral shades, printmaking paper is best. You can also buy blank cards, but be sure the paper stock is not too lightweight.

1 TEAR AN EDGE OR CUT A STRAIGHT EDGE. For a distressed look, use a ruler as a guide, and rip toward you. For clean, cut edges rather than the feathered edges that tearing produces, cut along the ruler with a rotary cutter.

2 SCORE THE FOLD. To make the center fold, use a bone folder (or any tool with a smooth, rounded end) to press and set the fold.

Create a Collage

Use bits of paper, fabric, ribbon, and trim for your collage. Japanese and art papers, pictures pulled from magazines, old calendars, postcards, and even paint chips will fit the bill. Add bits of velvet, silk, wool, and snazzy print fabrics for tactile quality and to add dimension. Then try out various arrangements before you commit to one and glue.

1 CUT OUT SOME SHAPES. Fringe fabric ends, and tear paper shapes for interest. With burnout velvet fabric, as shown at right, you can cut off the sheer backing.

2 GLUE IT ON. Spray your shapes with 505, or brush the shapes over your glue stick. Press them onto the paper. Lay a heavy book on top of the card while it dries.

3 STITCH DOWN. Use all of the fancy decorative stitches on your machine. With the right side facing up, sew over and around the fabrics and papers in a loose pattern.

4 ADD BEADS OR BUTTONS. Glue on three-dimensional objects: beads, buttons, or even shells and charms. If you plan to mail your card, make sure that the items will fit in your envelope and won't be crushed.

5 COVER THE STITCHES ON THE INSIDE. You might like the look of the stitching on the inside cover of your card. If not, simply glue a rectangle of decorative paper over it.

And the envelope please

If you don't have an envelope into which the new card will fit, just make one. Take apart an old envelope to use as a pattern.

1 TAKE APART AN OLD ENVELOPE. Enlarge or reduce the envelope across the width or length as needed. Trace it on decorative paper, and cut it out.

2 STITCH WHILE FLAT. If you're making an envelope, why not add some decorative stitching to it, too? Sew it while it's cut out but still flat and unglued. Then fold it, and glue.

tip

If you used a large button or delicate beads as accents, wrap the card in bubble wrap or tissue paper before you put it in an envelope.

Sole-ful Slippers

What better way to treat important people in your life than to give them a pair of handcrafted slippers? Happy feet equal happy folk, after all. Here, you'll find a straightforward step-by-step process for making fabric slippers (from fitting and patternmaking to stitching on a thin leather sole). The drawing below shows the parts of a typical slipper, and in the drawings on p. 23, there's a handful of slipper design sketches to get your own creative juices flowing. Together, these offerings should set you squarely on the path to making perfect slippers for all the heels and toes on your gift list.

SASKIA WASSING-SHEPHERD *wrote "Light on the Sole" in* Threads *issue 104.*

Supplies

- Paper and pencil
- Scissors
- Sewing machine
- Hand needle and thread
- Fabrics and lining
- Leather sole
- ¼-inch industrial wool felt
- Beacon's Fabri-Tac
- Inexpensive ½-inch brush
- Needle-nose pliers

THE PARTS

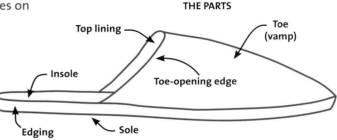

Make the patterns

Use the basic pattern on p. 24 as your starting point, or trace your friend's foot as described below to make a custom pattern.

1 TRACE THE SOLE. Standing barefoot on a piece of paper, trace around one foot. Cut out the template, and mark a center line the length of the template and a perpendicular line across its widest part. Make the sole pattern by placing the foot template on paper and drawing around it. Allow ⅛-inch ease on each side, except at the front, where you can draw any toe shape you want. Transfer the lines from the foot template to the sole.

2 DRAW THE TOP. Measure across the foot's widest point (B) and the arch (C). On paper placed under the sole pattern, extend lines B and C to match these measurements. To draw the curve, mark points E ½ inch below line C. Curve to a point about 1 inch above line E at the center. Connect the dots.

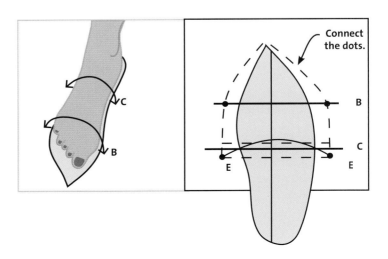

Sew the slippers

Use nylon or polyester thread; it's stronger than cotton thread.

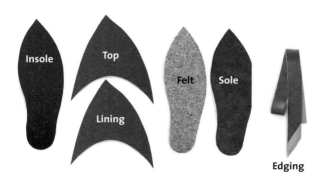

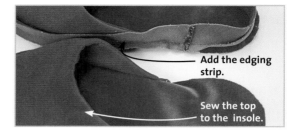

1 CUT OUT ALL THE PARTS. Adding ¼-inch seam allowances to all of the edges, mark and cut out the insoles, tops, and linings. (If using velvet or other fabric with pile, point the pile toward the heel.) Mark and cut the felt and leather soles without seam allowances. Remember to reverse the pattern for each foot! Cut two 1¼-inch-wide bias strips that are each long enough to fit around the outside edge of the sole, plus ½ inch.

2 SEW THE TOP TO THE INSOLE. Line each top by joining the lining and top right sides together along the opening edge. Turn it right-side out, and press. Starting at the toe point, pin and sew each side of the top to the insole with the top and the insole facing up.

3 ADD THE EDGING STRIP. With all edges aligned and fabric right sides together, pin the sole edging strip around the slipper, starting and ending at the inside arch. Sew from the underside, stitching just inside the previous stitches. Sew the edging ends together. Trim them to ⅛ inch.

Attach the felt

First make sure that the wool felt padding fits exactly within the insole seamline. Trim if needed.

1 GLUE THE INSOLE. Spread an even layer of Fabri-Tac on the wrong side of the insole inside the seamline only. Allow the Fabri-Tac to dry. (Fabri-Tac is clear; the blue here is for photographic purposes.

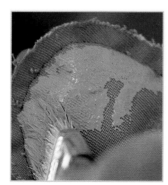

2 PRESS THE FELT IN PLACE. Also apply Fabri-Tac to the top side of the felt sole. Then press the two glued surfaces together firmly, starting at the heel and working up to the toe. Keep the felt inside the seamline, and smooth away any wrinkles or air pockets.

3 GLUE THE EDGING. Apply Fabri-Tac to the inside of the edging, catching the felt edge and both sides of all seam allowances. Don't apply Fabri-Tac to the outside ¼ inch of the edging, as shown. Then apply a ½-inch band of Fabri-Tac to the underside edge of the felt.

4 WRAP THE EDGING TO THE UNDERSIDE. Wrap the edging around the felt. Start at the front, miter corners, and distribute any excess evenly around curves. Keep pressing the edging down for a few minutes to ensure a good bond.

Add the leather sole

Trim the leather sole if necessary to fit exactly over the edged felt padding.

1 CLIP AWAY BULK. Clip any miters or excess overlaps so the edging lies flat.

2 GLUE THE LEATHER. Apply Fabri-Tac evenly to the underside of the sole leather and the felt up to ¼ inch from the outside edge of each. Allow it to dry. Then carefully attach the sole to the underside of the slipper, working from heel to toe. Press them together well to ensure a good, even bond.

3 STITCH THE SOLE TO THE EDGING. With a strong thread, sew around the leather's edge with a ¼-inch blanket stitch. Stitch through the leather and then through the edging instead of going through both at once. Use needle-nose pliers, if necessary, to get a firm grip on the needle.

Design to suit

The variety of possible materials is endless: velvets, satins, silks, wool felt, suede, shearling, denim, tapestry, brocades. Mix colors for contrast, or go with monochromatic designs. Also consider beaded details, appliqué designs, stenciling, embroidered monograms, and unusual trims.

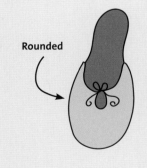

Rounded

Rounded pointy

Embroidered details

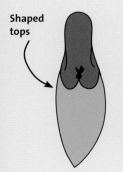

Shaped tops

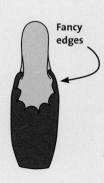

Fancy edges

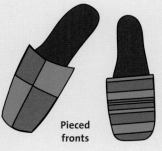

Pieced fronts

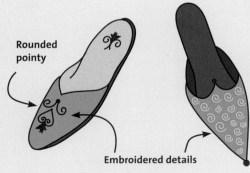

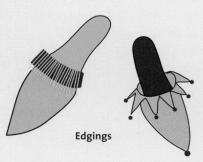

Edgings

Patterns & Template

Before making copies of any patterns or templates, check the accuracy of your photocopier by making one copy and comparing it to the original. Permission granted to copy patterns and templates for personal use.

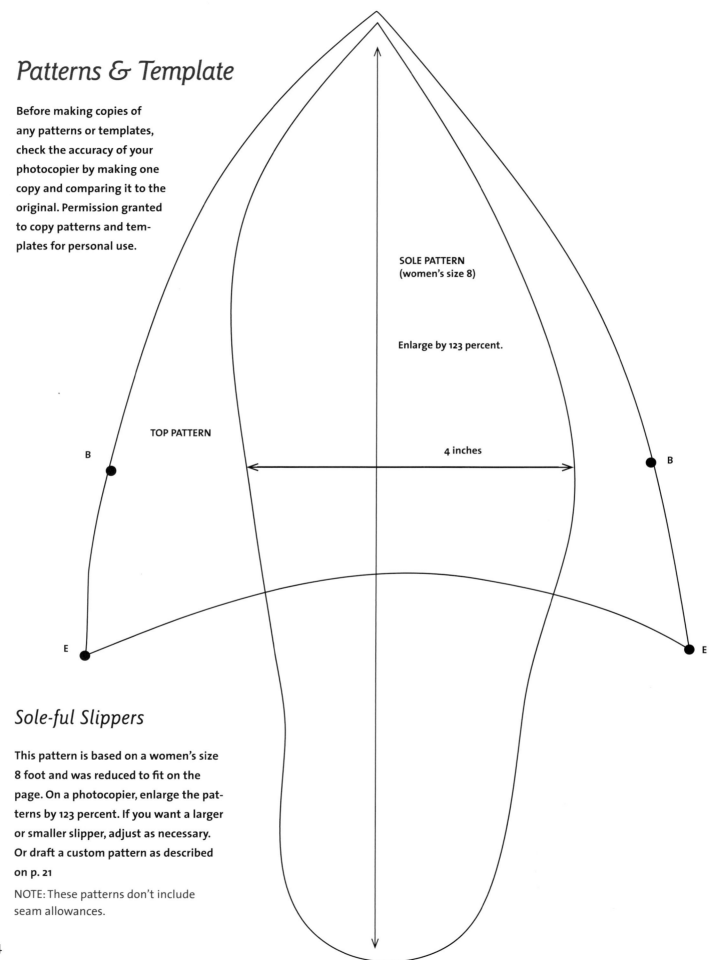

SOLE PATTERN
(women's size 8)

Enlarge by 123 percent.

TOP PATTERN

B

B

4 inches

E

E

Sole-ful Slippers

This pattern is based on a women's size 8 foot and was reduced to fit on the page. On a photocopier, enlarge the patterns by 123 percent. If you want a larger or smaller slipper, adjust as necessary. Or draft a custom pattern as described on p. 21

NOTE: These patterns don't include seam allowances.

Travel Accessories

Easy-to-construct and pretty to look at, these fabric bags keep undergarments organized and shoes protected. Practical to boot, the two-pocket lingerie bag can drape conveniently over a hanger, keeping clothes clean and right by your other garments, while the shoe bag features a center divider to prevent the bottom of one shoe from dirtying the top of the other. Any fabric will work, but choosing a mid- to heavyweight cotton fabric, such as matelassé or canvas for the exterior fabric and cotton muslin for the lining, makes these bags durable and easy to care for. These lovely bags are a cinch to sew and are great gifts for all your traveling friends.

JULIETTE LANVERS *sews in Salt Lake City, Utah. Chickpea-Studio.com.*

Sew a sweet lingerie bag

Two pockets meet in the center, and a flap closes the lingerie bag. While you're traveling, drape this bag over a hanger's horizontal bar to keep your delicates protected. When you're not traveling, place this bag in a drawer to keep things neat and organized.

Supplies

Both versions:
- 1½ yards home décor or bottom-weight fabric, such as matelassé or canvas
- 1½ yards muslin
- Polyester thread
- Ruler
- Water- or air-soluble fabric marker

Optional:
- Dinner plate , protractor, or other rounded template

tip **ADD EMBROIDERY**

Are you giving these bags as gifts? Embroider a motif or monogram letters for a personalized designer look. Add your design to the flap center before attaching the exterior fabric to the lining.

Use a rounded template, such as a dinner plate, to shape the flap edge.

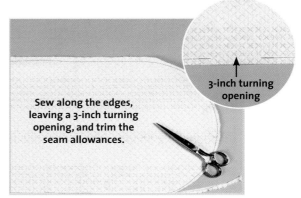

Sew along the edges, leaving a 3-inch turning opening, and trim the seam allowances.

3-inch turning opening

1 PREPARE THE FABRICS. Prewash the fabrics in the same way you plan to launder them in the future. Cut the exterior and the lining fabrics 11 inches by 43 inches.

2 SHAPE THE FLAP. With right sides together, align the exterior and lining fabrics. Using a protractor, a dinner plate, or other rounded template, draw a curved line along one short edge. Cut along the marked line. This rounded edge is the bag flap. Pin around the bag perimeter, right sides together.

3 ATTACH THE EXTERIOR AND THE LINING FABRICS. Sew around the bag edges with a ⅜-inch-wide seam allowance, leaving a 3-inch turning opening on one long side. Clip the corners and trim the curved edge seam allowance. Turn the fabric right side out, and press well.

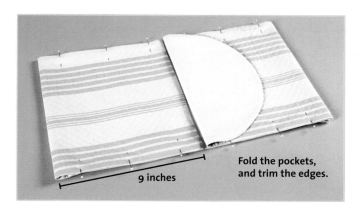

9 inches

Fold the pockets, and trim the edges.

Top-and edgestitch the pocket sides.

4 **FOLD THE POCKETS.** With the lining side up, fold up the straight short edge 9 inches. Fold down the rounded short edge approximately 15 inches. You are making two equal, 9-inch-deep pockets and a flap. Pin along the pocket sides without catching the flap.

5 **SEW THE EDGES.** Topstitch along the pocket sides with a ¼-inch seam allowance, leaving the flap free. Sew the seams a second time ⅛ inch from the edge, and press the seams.

Make a stylish shoe bag

The shoe bag is a variation on the lingerie bag. You'll sew a larger pocket and split it to create a separate compartment for each shoe.

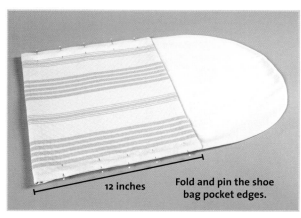

12 inches

Fold and pin the shoe bag pocket edges.

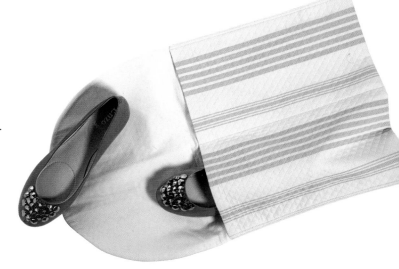

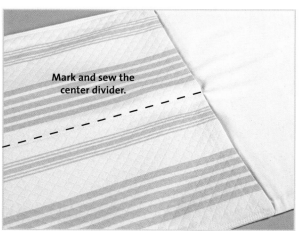

Mark and sew the center divider.

1 **PREPARE THE FABRICS.** Prewash the fabrics in the same way you plan to launder them in the future. Cut the exterior and the lining fabrics 15 inches by 36 inches.

2 **FOLLOW THE LINGERIE BAG.** Steps 2 and 3, on page 25.

3 **FOLD THE POCKET.** Place the sewn piece on the table, lining side up. Fold over the straight short edge 12 inches, and pin along the sides. The curved edge is the flap.

4 **FOLLOW THE LINGERIE BAG.** Step 5, above

5 **MARK THE CENTER DIVIDER.** With a ruler, mark the middle of the pocket with a temporary pen to create two equal compartments. Pin all layers of the pocket in a few places, and sew along the line.

Textile Triangles

The gift box has taken on a new look. With four sides and four points, these textile tetrahedrons could be called "perpetual gift tents," but no matter what you call them, there are countless ways in which you can use them. Their hollow bellies are perfect to bear small gifts year after year, and their unique frames make them just as giftworthy when empty as they are when they're full.

Make a large padded one for your cat to sleep in, or add a handle, and carry it like a purse. Hang it from a holiday tree, or leave it underneath for someone special. Use them to hold potpourri or lavender. Once you get the knack for sewing these fabric containers, you'll find they go together very quickly—with a nifty little zipper trick, too.

JUDITH NEUKAM *is senior technical editor of* Threads *magazine.*

Supplies

- Fabric
- Hand needle
- Heavyweight fusible interfacing
- Zipper
- Tassel
- Thread
- Scissors
- Sewing machine
- Lining fabric

Here's the angle

Use the pattern on p. 31, and enlarge or reduce it as desired. Then cut, mark, and sew your fabric as shown below. Note that you use only half of the zipper for a unique U-turn application.

1 CUT AND INTERFACE YOUR RECTANGLE. Fuse the wrong side of your fabric rectangle with a heavyweight fusible interfacing. Baste ⅝ inch from the edges. Fold the rectangle in half, and chalk the triangle pattern on both sides.

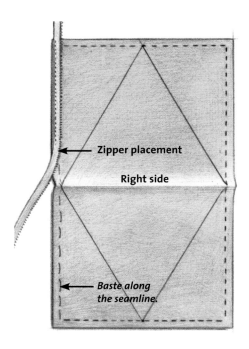

Zipper placement

Right side

Baste along the seamline.

2 EDGESTITCH THE TRIANGLE. To create crisp edges, fold the fabric along the triangle outlines one edge at a time, and edgestitch (sew ¹⁄₁₆ inch from the fold) from point to point.

PREPARE A NYLON ZIPPER. The zipper should be at least 2 inches longer than the long edge of the fabric. Pry the metal stops off the top and bottom, open the zipper, and remove the slider. Set the slider aside.

ATTACH THE ZIPPER. Place the fabric right-side up. Center half of the zipper right-side down on the basted edge, aligning the teeth with the stitches and the zipper tape over the seam allowance. Sew the tape to the fabric. Then fold the seam allowance and the zipper to the wrong side along the basting line. Topstitch through all of the layers.

Finishing Touches

There are many options for finishing your textile triangle.

BOTTOM SUPPORT
If the triangle is large and the fabric is heavy, cut a bottom insert from a ½-inch-thick sheet of foam rubber, buckram, or heavy felt. Tack it to the seam allowances after the box is made.

LINING
For a smooth finish inside, cut a lining the same shape as your pattern. Sew it into the seam with the zipper. Sew the opposite seam separately with right sides together. Then complete the construction at left, treating the two layers as one.

ZIPPER-PULL DECORATION
Snazz up the zipper pull with tassels, ribbons, charms, beads, recycled jewelry, or hand-sewn gift tags.

3 REPLACE THE SLIDER. With right sides together, fold the rectangle in half at the zipper midpoint. Ease the zipper ends back into the slider. Close the zipper, and make sure that the pull sits at the fabric fold. Sew the edge opposite the zipper, as shown at right.

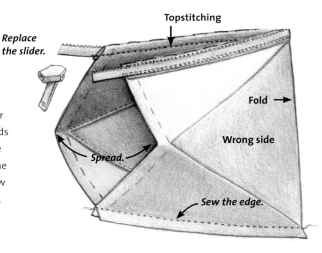

Replace the slider.

Topstitching

Fold

Wrong side

Spread.

Sew the edge.

4 SEW IT CLOSED. Open the zipper halfway so you'll be able to turn the triangle right-side out later. Refold the fabric so that the zipper is centered, as shown at right. Sew the last edge. Turn it right-side out.

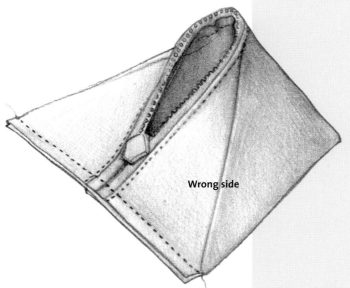

Wrong side

Patterns & Template

Crescent Clutch, p. 14

For the clutch pattern: Enlarge each pattern piece 400 percent. For a medium-sized clutch, enlarge the pattern pieces 300 percent, and for a wallet-size clutch, enlarge them 200 percent. Permission granted to copy patterns and templates for personal use.

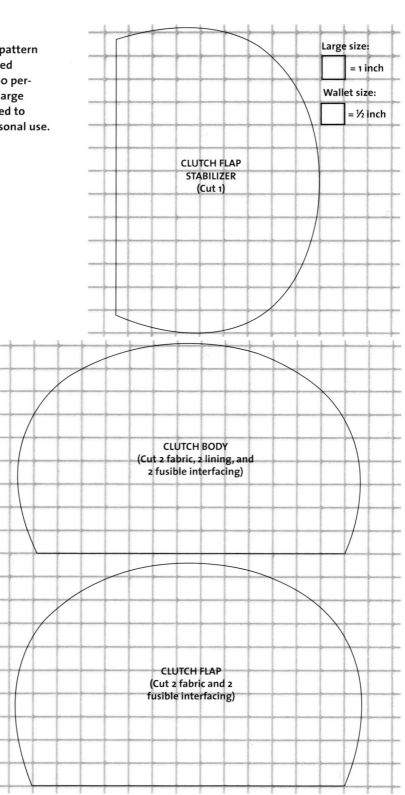

Large size:

◻ = 1 inch

Wallet size:

◻ = ½ inch

CLUTCH FLAP
STABILIZER
(Cut 1)

CLUTCH BODY
(Cut 2 fabric, 2 lining, and
2 fusible interfacing)

CLUTCH FLAP
(Cut 2 fabric and 2
fusible interfacing)

Textile Triangles, p. 28

On a photocopier, enlarge this pattern at 185 percent to produce a 3D triangle with a 6-inch base. You can enlarge or reduce the pattern to create a collection of different-sized triangles, as shown on p. 28. Permission granted to copy patterns and templates for personal use.

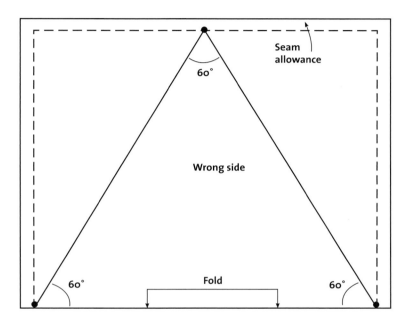

Credits

Many of the projects, patterns, and photos in this booklet have appeared previously in issues of *Threads*, *SewStylish*, and/or *CraftStylish*. Listed here are the author, photographer, and *Threads* issue # or publication title.

Easy Beaded Bags
Debbie Corson. Photos: Sloan Howard. Stylist: Jessica Saal. *SewStylish*, Winter 2009

Pretty Pin Cushions
Jen Segrest. Completed Pincushions Photos: Scott Phillips. Stylist: Jessica Saal. All other photos: Sloan Howard. *SewStylish*, Holiday 2007

Origami Pouches
Adapted from *Threads* article "Mini Purses" by Paddye Mann. Photos: Sloan Howard. Stylist: Jessica Saal. Illustrations: Kat Riehle. *Threads* #134

Pillow Pom-Poms
Nicole Smith. Photos: Zach DeSart and Burcu Avsar. *Craftstylish*, Vol. VI

Crescent Clutch
Erika Kern (Etsy.com/Shop/MyImaginaryBoyfriend). Photos: Sloan Howard. Stylist: Jessica Saal. Illustrations: Kat Riehle. *SewStylish*, Winter 2011

Collage Cards Galore
Chris Timmons. Completed Card Photos: Scott Phillips. All Other Photos: Sloan Howard. Stylist: Jessica Saal. *SewStylish*, Holiday 2007

Sole-ful Slippers
Adapted from *Threads* article "Light On the Sole" by Saskia Wassing-Shepherd. Step-by-Step Photos: David Page Coffin. All Other Photos: Scott Phillips. "The Parts" Illustration: Karen Meyer. "Draw the Top" illustration: Saskia-Wassing-Shepherd. "Design to Suit" Illustrations: Katharina Riehle. *Threads* #104

Travel Accessories
Juliette Lanvers (ChickpeaStudio.com). Photos: Sloan Howard. Stylist: Jessica Saal. *SewStylish*, Winter 2012

Textile Triangles
Judith Neukam. Photos: Scott Phillips. Illustrations: Bob LaPointe. *SewStylish*, Holiday 2007